Authorpreneur in Pajamas:

Building Your Author's Platform Without Leaving Your Home

Geraldine Solon

"Authorpreneur in Pajamas" is an inspirational guide for aspiring authors. It provides the beginning fiction writer with ideas to take their first steps to publishing their work."
Marsha Collier bestselling author of *eBay for Dummies* and *Forbes* Top Ten Social Media Influencers

Copyright © 2014, Geraldine Solon
All Rights Reserved

ISBN: 978-1495201677

PRINTED IN THE UNITED STATES OF AMERICA

To all the authors and aspiring authors around the world, may you continue to grow and shine in your career.

Introduction

Next to motherhood, I personally believe that being an author is the best job in the world. I chose to write this book because when I started marketing my novels, I had to learn the ropes all by myself. I didn't have the faintest clue about building my author's platform, but I knew that my journey of learning and growth would be significant for new authors. I knew I needed to set aside my creative hat and think like an entrepreneur. Building my author's platform took three months, and I haven't stopped growing and evolving. After presenting at various events, writers have requested that I write a book on how I built my author's platform.

I do believe that an author should have a strong presence in person and online. What makes this book different from the rest is that I focus on how authors can promote themselves online. We live in a virtual world, where digital has taken over paper, where smart phones, tablets and eReaders are now necessities, and where you can get the word out there in seconds.

This is the best time to be an author. Whether you're published through a traditional publishing house or are self-published, you still have to work hard to build your author's platform. As of today, more authors are choosing to publish their book themselves. Reasons include being able to have full control of their work and not having to wait years until their book is released. There has been a spurt of freelance graphic designers, cover artists, and editors who are offering their services to authors. The royalties go directly into the author's pocket with no middle men involved. A stream of independent authors are now Kindle Millionaires. Indie authors are pricing their eBooks much lower than traditionally published books. This has proven to be an effective marketing strategy for them to entice readers. Readers have discovered notable talent from Indie authors who had the courage to publish their books.

2011 was a phenomenal year for Indie Authors. The closing of Borders and Barnes and Noble bookstores raised the demand for eReaders, and many bold authors embraced the Indie movement. The Amazon Kindle became the most sought after eReader after they launched their first Kindle in 2007. The gadget was reasonably priced, and consumers found it more convenient to download a book versus purchasing a hard copy. In terms of pricing point, eBooks became more affordable than paperbacks and hard bound books.

Amazon is a major player in the Indie movement. They witnessed the demand in authors wanting to independently publish their books without paying upfront fees. They offered authors the option of having eBooks in a Kindle format, and launched Createspace which allowed authors to produce a paperback at no cost to the author. Soon Barnes and Noble introduced the Nook tablet which gave readers the option to read in color. Independent Silicon Valley eBook publishers, Smashwords and Scribd gave authors the opportunity of uploading their books in different electronic formats without paying a fee. Amazon is now a major publisher.

Virtual blog tours have taken over conventional face-to-face book signings. Book reviewers and bloggers can post reviews on their blogs and other sites. With the birth of social media like Facebook, Twitter, and Goodreads, authors can easily promote their books without leaving their home. Fans wanting autograph copies of their favorite authors can now use Kindlegraph for a virtual autograph.

Books, movies, and other forms of entertainment will always be there. The method of delivery may not be as conventional as we're used to, but they shall always be a part of our life. So this leads me to conclude that we live in an era of options and opportunities, where change is inevitable, and now is the best time to be an author. The virtual world is endless. Embrace it!

Chapter 1
Why Do You Write?

Being a new author can be intimidating. You're exposing a piece of yourself and may be fearful to take that first leap. The first question you need to ask yourself is why do you write?

Do you write to make money? As you may know, there are a lot of starving writers. Do you write because it makes you happy and you want to follow your passion? Do you have a message you wish to share with the world? Do you wish to find healing?

All of the above are valid questions that will determine your goal. Once you have a clearer sense of where you're going, you'll have a greater understanding on how to build your author's platform and target the right audience.

The second factor you need to key in is if you're writing as a hobby or as a career. If you're writing as a hobby then your goals differ from someone who is writing as a career. Writing as a hobby has no pressure. You may be writing for a select group of people like friends and family. Those who write as a hobby are eager to collect stories. On the other hand, if you're writing as a career, you're most likely to spend time honing your craft. An author serious about his/her work will read constantly, invest in resources and be committed to writing.

Hard core authors are determined about their craft, and they know that building a brand entails hard work. They eat, breathe and live their writing.

Chapter 2
Identify Who Your Readers Are

Most authors hope to reach a wide audience with their books. However, the majority of authors don't realize that they should know who their readers will be before writing their book. If you're writing a non-fiction book about the global economy then most likely your readers will be economists, business owners and world leaders. If you're writing a children's book then you must first establish the age group of your readers. If you're writing a futuristic novel set in a different world/realm or a dystopian novel, then most likely you'll have young adult and adult readers. If you're writing a self-help book about parenting, then you know that your readers will be parents, upcoming parents, and people who fill the role of parents.

Your readers should be classified by age group, gender, and niche. For fiction authors, books are divided by genre. If you're writing a romance novel, a majority of your readers will be women in their twenties and above, while if you write thrillers or mysteries, you'll get a combination of both men and women. Targeting who your readers are early on will assist you with your marketing strategy.

If you're not sure who your readers are, look at the online bookstores like Amazon or Barnes and Noble and search for books that are similar to yours. You can read the first chapters of their books and based on that, you'll have an idea of where to classify your book.

Chapter 3
What is an Authorpreneur?

An Authorpreneur focuses on establishing one's brand to the consumer using different avenues to promote their work.

A platform is what defines your visibility with your audience. Are people aware of your existence? What avenues do you use to keep people informed about you and your book? Is what you're offering credible enough for people to grasp? Are you influential enough to convince people that your book is worthwhile? Are you targeting the right audience for your work?

As an Authorpreneur who is building one's platform online, the first thing you need to think of is image. What do you want readers to know about you? Platform is not about selling your books, but about being an authority in your field. What impression do you want to leave with your readers and fans? Please note that building a platform doesn't happen overnight. It's similar to a song which starts as a crescendo and takes months to build. Once you've built your platform, you have to continue growing it to reach a wider audience.

The publishing market changes all the time, and you can't be complacent. An Authorpreneur is someone who is on top of the game, always learning new things and willing to be innovative. An Authorpreneur will never stop researching and reaching out to his/her audience and fans.

Chapter 4
You Published Your Book, Now What?

Most authors are giddy and on top of the world after seeing their book published. If you have a paperback version, I can guarantee that most of you have smelled your book, taken lots of pictures and uploaded to your Facebook page. But the million dollar question every author faces is, "How am I going to sell my book?

With fifteen hundred books released every day, what will make your book stand out from the rest? Writing a damn good book which has been professionally edited and sports an eye-catching book cover is only the icing on the cake. You need to be able to inform people that your book is available. You've worked sleepless nights while presuming that your task is complete after typing, *The End*. I hate to tell you this, but the work is definitely not over. In fact, you've only just begun. Be ready for another long sleepless season with lots of hard work, blood, sweat, and tears.

New authors often ask why they have to market their book. They wonder why their books can't sell by itself. First and foremost, if you're writing as a hobby and only intend to sell your books to your sweet grandmother or your classmate from fifth grade, then this book isn't for you. Statistics show that only seven percent of authors sell more than a thousand books. That's right, seven percent! So what ever happened to the ninety three percent? You guessed it right. . .They all thought their work was done and somewhere down the road, their book would make it to the hands of thousands of readers. This is no fairytale, and if you're thinking of growing your career as an author, then this book is for you.

From a woman's perspective, pretend that you're preparing for your wedding day. You have ninety days to plan your wedding and want your event to be stellar. You're already getting the jitters and running around like a headless chicken. All the wedding details keep haunting you late at night and you can't sleep. Will the flowers match your elegant dress? Should the cake be vanilla or chocolate? What colors should the invitations be? Will you be inviting your old roommate from college? Are you ready to face your overpowering mother-in-law, and most of all, will the wedding day be perfect?

From a man's perspective, picture this project as a job promotion. Your boss has a list of candidates that are eligible for promotion, and each of you have ninety days to prove to your boss that you're the right one. What steps will you take? Will you come to work extra early and leave much later during the day? Will you be more creative in closing that next deal or winning that potential client? At the end of the day, what will it entail for your boss to choose you?

This all boils down to marketing, selling yourself, building your author's platform and convincing everyone that you are the next best thing. I chose ninety days, because this is how long it took to build my author's platform. When I released my first novel, *Love Letters,* in January 2011, I didn't have a clue how to market my novel. Like any naïve, first-time author, I believed my book was magically going to reach as many readers as I want without me lifting a finger. I only sold five books in the first month and this was through friends and relatives. In the next month, I doubled in sales and the succeeding months generated more, but I was not content with the numbers. That's when I began researching everyday what I needed to do to build my author's platform.

In July 2011, I released my second book, *Chocolicious*, and after ninety days, voila. *Chocolicious* became a best-seller on Amazon. *Chocolicious* ranked #69 in the overall Top 100 Amazon eBook list and made it to top five of several categories. *Love Letters* made it to overall Top 100 best-seller list as well ranking #75. I was selling more than a thousand books a day and in that month alone, I sold more books than I sold in a lifetime.

This isn't a book about how to become a best-seller. This book is about how to build your author's platform without leaving your home. Building your author's platform involves a lot of hard work, patience, and determination. I will confess that at times building an author's brand can take you away from your writing, but this mostly happens during the initial stages. Once you've built your platform, you'll have gained a list of loyal fans that will follow you throughout your career. If you're willing to work hard, all you need is the courage and determination to fulfill your goals. I will show you the steps I took to build my platform and how you can do this at the pleasure of not having to leave your home while you connect globally with people online.

Chapter 5
Even Shy People Can Sell Their Books Online

I love meeting people. I often speak at events and conduct book signings. It helps to have that extrovert personality, but not every author wants to go out and meet people to talk about their work. A lot of authors prefer to hide behind their computer as they create a world of their own mingling with their imaginary friends. When it's time to market their book, the anxiety creeps in and they don't have the courage to promote their book face-to-face. We live in a digital age where you can acquire virtual friends and followers without meeting them in person

There are numerous opportunities and resources that authors can tap into without leaving their own home. It can be three o'clock in the morning and you're still up wearing your pajamas while trying to promote your book. Nobody can see what you're wearing, or they won't know if you're having a bad hair day. You can use the magic of words to sell and promote your book.

The beauty of doing everything online is you can cut through all the chase of getting dolled up, driving to an event and having a set schedule. Working in your pajamas provides you the luxury of having your own schedule. Nobody is there to judge you. You are in control of what you produce online and want readers to see.

One advantage of promoting yourself online is that you are in charge of the message you want to deliver to your audience. This also means you have to be careful what you're producing online.

Chapter 6
Sales and Marketing Are From Different Planets

There's a big reason why marketing and sales come from different planets. Although they work well together, it's vital to plan your strategy before you sell your book. Sales is all about selling the finished product. Marketing is composed of packaging, pricing, quality control and ensuring that your product is ready for the world to see. Some new authors complain when they believe they've written a good book but can't sell it. The first thing I ask them is, "Have you marketed your work?" They look at me with eyebrows creased, not comprehending what I just said. As you see, marketing involves a lot of creative thinking.

As authors, we need to think outside the box and make an effort to spread the word about our book. One thing I believe is to never underestimate yourself. Your book could be worth a fortune if you know how to package your work. Ask yourself, what is the best way to reach out to your readers?

Every author should make investments in presentation. Invest in yourself. You are your greatest product and behind every book lies an author who wrote it. You have to be the first and topmost investment. You want readers to be drawn to you, and investing in a high-resolution photo demands a priority. You might be the next most sought after author hitting the New York Times bestseller list, but choosing not to invest in a headshot photo reveals unprofessionalism. Most press releases require a press kit which includes a professional photo not taken with your Smartphone.

Imagine a chef competing in a culinary event where they will be judged for presentation, creativity, cohesiveness and taste. As you can see, the food may taste delicious but if the chef didn't work hard to creatively present his food, you know exactly what the judges will think. Creating a first impression takes seven seconds so you have to give it your best shot.

Investing in a cover artist should be a priority. A spellbinding cover captures the eye. As Helen of Troy had a face that could launch a thousand ships, wouldn't you want your cover to launch a thousand readers? Some cover artists could be costly but think of your cover as an investment. You can also check free stock photos online to use for your book cover. We live in a visual world, and if your cover doesn't stand out from the rest, what incentive will you provide your readers to take that second look? To gain ideas, study the covers of your favorite authors. Your cover has to resonate with you.

Hook your readers head on with a notable summary. You don't want to waste their time, and you need to capture their attention in the first sentence alone. Keep the summary to two hundred fifty words. Invest in marketing materials like bookmarks, business cards and virtual banners to promote your work.

Chapter 7
Research is a Must

Did you see that commercial from AT&T of the guy dancing in the subway? He received a text message late because his phone wasn't 4G. An author can feel this way when he doesn't research about the publishing industry. With all the changes in the publishing industry, authors should strive to keep up to date. I spend two hours each day researching online to find effective ways to build my platform. There are a lot of opportunities and resources offered online, and you want to be able to spot those gems.

As I mentioned earlier, an Authorpreneur needs to be on top of the game and ahead of the crowd. An Authorpreneur should be a leader who creates trends. As a new author, where do you start? When I released my first book, I perused websites of my favorite authors and read every single page. Since these authors inspired me so much, I wanted to verify what they were doing and how I can effectively build my platform. Most of my favorite authors are published through the prominent publishing houses, and I'm aware that they have their publicists to assist them with their promotions. However, that never stopped me from researching. Every day, I told myself that I needed to learn tips to increase my exposure. I read every blog about writing, publishing and marketing every single day as most of this information is available online.

The internet offers a ton of information and resources that will take you to various avenues of promoting your work.

Resources:
http://www.writersdigest.com/
http://pred-ed.com/
http://agentquery.com/
http://absolutewrite.com/
http://calwriters.org/
http://alanrinzler.com/
http://author-network.com/
http://www.wow-womenonwriting.com/
http://passionatepen.com/
http://www.nathanbransford.com/
http://www.publishersmarketplace.com/
http://www.pw.org/
http://cba-ramblings.blogspot.com/
http://janefriedman.com/blog/
http://queryshark.blogspot.com/
http://pubrants.blogspot.com/
http://www.shewrites.com/
http://redroom.com/
http://squawvalleywriters.org/

http://sfwriters.org/
http://www.novel-writing-help.com/
http://www.ninetydegreesmedia.com/
http://www.noveladvice.com.
http://www.fictionwriters.com
http://www.authorlink.com
http://www.publaw.com
http://www.pen.org
http://www.bartleby.com
http://www.larsen-pomada.com
http://www.allaboutlove.net/
http://amherstwriters.com/
http://novelmatters.blogspot.com/
http://pubmission.com/
http://www.womensliteraryfestival.com/
http://fwwriters.algonkianconferences.com/
http://www.bookpassage.com/
http://www.napawritersconf.org/
http://www.mcwc.org/
http://slolibraryfoundation.org/CCBAF2.html
http://writeandpitchconference.com/
http://www.squawvalleywriters.org/
http://www.svrwa.com/
http://www.scribd.com/
http://www.smashwords.com/
https://www.createspace.com/
http://www.lulu.com/
http://chipmacgregor.typepad.com/
http://www.blockbusterplots.com/
http://offthebookshelf.com/
http://www.thewritersjourney.com/
http://chrisvogler.wordpress.com/
http://www.thepassionatewriter.com/
http://www.sfwa.org/for-authors/writer-beware/

http://www.suite101.com/
http://www.RomanceNovelEditor.com
http://writers.net/
http://www.kensingtonbooks.com/
http://dorchesterpub.com/
http://www.avonromance.com/

Chapter 8
Competition is Healthy

Competition has taught me a lot about branding myself. I spend time watching authors who write the same genre as I do and study what I can do differently from them. I write Women's fiction and Romance novels which are known to be a competitive market. Seventy-five percent of the readers are women. Top authors like Nicholas Sparks, Danielle Steel, and Kristin Hannah have proven to be successful. You don't want to follow their style, but you can gain tips on finding your voice and packaging yourself so readers can identify with your work. Studying the marketing strategies of these authors has assisted me with my career. Non-fiction authors also have to provide a clear topic of what they're writing about. There are many experts in the field, and being authentic and having the authority to write your topic will assist you in standing out from the rest.

Investigate the methods these authors use to promote themselves. Who are their audience? You would want to target them. What are they doing differently? Why do readers want to read their work? This all boils down to your brand and how you want your readers to identify with you. Every author needs to share a piece of them. Writing fiction entails an emotional journey. You don't want to stay stuck on your comfort zone. The possibilities of using your imagination are endless, and you need to show your readers that you're willing to take risks.

Show your readers that you don't only write about things you know. You may have a similar horror story like Stephen King, but yours has a twist based on the haunted ancestral home you grew up in. Showing a piece of you emanates your vulnerability. I mostly write about the things I care about, my deepest fears and the human condition. Readers will relate to your story if you reveal a vulnerable side of yourself.

As writers, we tend to collect stories, and nothing could be more enriching and heartfelt than when you write about your joy and pain. This divulges a more authentic you. If you try to follow the trend, then you're not original and only think about making money. After *Twilight* was released, so many people wrote about vampires and werewolves to keep up with the trend. There's nothing wrong with writing about that topic, but what makes Stephanie Meyers original is she took the vampire characters into a whole new level and made them the good guys.

If you're writing non-fiction and your book

mimics other self-help books, ask yourself what can you do differently.

When I started writing this book, I became a bit wary to complete the pages and feared that I wouldn't be able to compete with other marketing books. But when I decided I'd only focus on the theme of promoting online and never having to leave home, I knew I had an edge. My book would not be as similar to the rest of the marketing books. Given the fact that I used these strategies to promote my novels, I believe new authors would be willing to try what I did.

If you keep following all the rules, you lose out in using your imagination to the highest level. If you want your story to be memorable and endearing, you have to take yourself to that profound level and write from the heart.

Again, competition is healthy, but what will make you different from the rest? That's one way of branding yourself.

Chapter 9
Who Doesn't Love Bargains

Are you one of those bargain hunters who examine the store searching for clearances? I know I'm one of them, and tell me who doesn't love buying something that has more value than what you paid for. The same goes for your book. If you're independently published or traditionally published, you can work with your publisher to lower your price for a certain time period. If you have several books, try offering half off, or partner with another author and do a buy two for the price of one. That sweetens the deal even more.

If you're an Indie author that has your book published through Amazon and other online retailers, you can schedule a price change every so often. I usually schedule mine every three months to keep the momentum going. I keep the promo for two days and then bring back the original price. I have discovered that this tactic works and provides more exposure to my novels.

One tip would be to partner with another author or several authors who write in the same genre like you to sell your books at a bargain price for a few days. Did you ever notice that the back pages of your favorite author's book features books of other authors? This presents an excellent marketing strategy. Every reader reading that author's book will now see the cover of your book. Add a summary and first chapter to hook your readers to buy your book. Coordinating with a few authors allows you to promote their work with your readers and vice versa.

Chapter 10
Every Author Should Have a Website

Congratulations! You're now a published author ready to share your book with the world. Every author needs to possess a website. Your website says a lot about your identity and how you want your readers to perceive you. Choose themes and colors wisely, and use your name for your website. If you're using a pen name for your books then use the same name for your website. I use www.geraldinesolon.com since that's my name and the name I use for my books.

If readers need to find you, what better way to have all your information than on your website. Some authors use the name of their books as the website. That could work for them, but if you've written more than one book, it's essential to keep it under your name. Ideally, it's better to have your own domain name, although I know other authors who use a blog for their website or they combine both blog and website. Whatever works for you is fine as long as people know where to find you.

Your website is a reflection of who you are. Choose the designs and concepts wisely. Be true to the colors that you love. A website portrays your brand as an author. Keep your website informative and entertaining.

Your website needs to have the following:

1. **Welcome page**- This is the most important page of your website. How you create this page, will determine if the viewers want to peek at the other pages. I would suggest you add all the important highlights and latest announcements about your book on this page. Keep it simple and free from clutter. Many times, people visiting your website might only stop at this page. What a pity if you didn't have the information listed here. This page should be updated frequently to keep it fresh and up to date.
2. **Bio**- This is where you can feature your credentials, awards you won and anything you'd like to share with the public.
3. **Photo**- Your picture must be a professional looking one and not some random photo taken from your smartphone. Remember, you are your best asset and this should be together with your Bio.
4. **Books**- The purpose of having a website is to display your books. You'll want to hook your readers with the summary of your books and book covers.

5. **Contact Page-** Make sure that your contact info provides a means for people to contact you.

There are a lot of hosting sites that have templates for you to choose from.
You can buy domain names at:
Vistaprint.com
Godaddy.com
Free websites without domain names are from blogspot.com and wordpress.com

Chapter 11
Blogging Ain't Rocket Science

A blog is a website where you post journal entries about a specific topic. Most authors have their blogs on their website, while others keep them separate. Either way should be fine as long as people know where to find you. Although I don't blog actively, I know a lot of authors who do. Blogging may be difficult to balance when you're already writing and promoting books, but authors have discovered a way to maintain their blogs. Gathering content three months before you launch should keep you going, because I can guarantee that you will get burnt out. You don't have to post everyday. I know authors who post two to three times a week and have written their blogs ahead of time. When you ran out of content, you can have other authors or readers guest post on your blog.

Your posts don't always have to pertain to writing, editing, or promoting. You also want to connect to a bigger audience and portray a different side about you. Blogging should not overwhelm you, but it should allow you to inform, entertain and reach out to the community. If you follow a list of bloggers, they're most likely to follow you back. The key to promoting your blog is to add keywords of your themes and topics.

These free blog sites provide user-friendly templates.

Blogger

Wordpress

Be sure to follow other people's blogs. By following them you can keep up to date with their postings and gain more information of what's happening in the publishing industry.

Top Blogs That I Follow:
http://writerunboxed.com/
http://www.livewritethrive.com/
http://janefriedman.com/blog/
http://www.alanrinzler.com/blog/
http://jodyhedlund.blogspot.com/
http://www.rachellegardner.com/
http://www.thepassivevoice.com/
http://sethgodin.typepad.com/
http://jakonrath.blogspot.com/
http://www.thebookdesigner.com/
http://www.amarketingexpert.com/blog/
http://warriorwriters.wordpress.com/
http://www.thecreativepenn.com/blog/
http://www.therenegadewriter.com/
http://www.makealivingwriting.com/
http://socialmediajustforwriters.com/

You can boost exposure by participating in a

virtual blog tour. A virtual blog tour is an online campaign wherein an author is featured as a guest in different blog. A virtual blog tour is scheduled consecutively for a week or more with up to 7-14 blogs scheduled ahead of time. With so many bookstores closing, authors have had to innovate and think of non-conventional book launches.

With the power of technology, you can schedule a virtual book tour with just a click of a button. There are thousands of book reviewers who read books from different genres and post an honest review on their blog. A few of the review sites are: GoodReads, Amazon, Barnes & Noble, Shelfari, and Library Thing. Most of these reviewers have hundreds of followers who will hear about your book. In return, they spread the word to their family and friends. They're still using the good old-fashioned word of mouth, only this time it is done virtually.

The author can do numerous promotions in a blog. A featured interview between blog host and author is one way for readers and fans to get to know who the author is. A guest post is where the author writes an article of their choice: usually pertaining to the craft of writing, editing or marketing as ways to offer tips and advice to new writers. Book give-aways and contests are popular ways to keep the virtual blog tours going. There are thousands of blogs available online, and you can either schedule a tour with organizers or do it yourself to save money.

Scheduling blog tours that focus on your books can be favorable for authors, but appearing in other blogs that spotlight different topics can also cater to a wider audience. As an author, you may have other interests aside from writing, and this is your opportunity to show a different side of yourself. If you're a dog lover and are willing to write an article about your 4 legged child, you'll not only reach dog lovers, but dog lovers who will want to read your books and tell their friends about your work. Contact the virtual bloggers ahead of time to schedule the dates.

Resources:
http://www.pumpupyourbook.com/tag/virtual-blog-tour/
http://www.virtualbooktourcafe.com/
http://www.wow-womenonwriting.com/
http://www.worldliterarycafe.com/
http://www.orangeberrybooktours.com/

Chapter 12
Virtual Book Clubs Create a Friendlier Place

Book clubs in the past were a form of social gatherings where a small group of readers would meet at bookstores, coffee shops or people's houses to discuss a book they've selected to read for the month. This became a popular trend when Oprah created her book club. A virtual book club on the other hand works the same way except you don't meet face to face. There are countless online book clubs that you can peruse, and the best is to get involved in a social network called, GoodReads.

GoodReads has a growing community that connects authors and readers. There has been a rise of virtual book clubs, where members can discuss their views online. Having your book chosen in a book club is one of the most rewarding feelings. You get to hear first hand how emotionally involved people are with your characters. In return, your readers can share the books with their friends and family. This means more exposure for your books. There are thousands of book clubs online with happy readers wanting to receive free electronic copies of your book. They will be your followers who can provide honest feedback.

Some authors have a reading guide in the back of their book. A reading guide with questions about each chapter can be used as a form of discussion for the members of a book club. Members also have their own random questions that they can ask authors.

Even if your book doesn't get selected in a book club, participating in one can build relationships with your peers. They will discover you're an author and will want to read your book.

With conventional book signings, authors could autograph their books to add that personal touch. Thanks to Autograph.com, authors can continue to autograph their eBooks through a digital signature which is automatically sent to the reader's device.

Chapter 13
Social Media is a Cool Place to Hangout

I truly believe in the power of social media. Social media has not only proven to be beneficial in my career but has also been very rewarding in terms of meeting people.

I attended a class on social media two years ago, and one basic factor I learned is that social media should focus on generosity. Social media provides an avenue to build your platform which is not in the form of hard selling to people to buy your book. There are many advantages of being active in social media and one of them is to remind you that you're not alone. As authors, we spend so much time typing on our computer that a majority of us yearn for that human contact.

We need to know that we're not alone in this journey, that there are other authors like us we can connect with, that there are valuable resources we can tap into and that there are readers and fans out there who can help us with our career.

Social media can be overwhelming if you don't have the time. Each social media venue plays a different role. The vital part is how you communicate and reach out to others. What may work for one, may not work for the other. My advice is to stick to one or two sites and learn to master the game.

Facebook:
When Facebook took the world by storm, almost everyone jumped on the band wagon and found long-lost friends. People were eager to catch up and rebuild their connections. I've heard stories of children who have been searching for their biological parents and were able to find them on Facebook. There are others who have rekindled an old flame with a long-lost love. There are countless stories where people have bonded together to raise funds for a good cause. Everybody has a story to tell when it comes to Facebook.

If you want to make an announcement or ask a question to a lot of people, then all you have to do is post a shout out on your Facebook wall. Amazing isn't it? If you want to show your friends the latest photos of your baby, you can just share it on Facebook. You're guaranteed to receive a response from your followers. This can be an ego booster for shy people, knowing you're not alone and you have people cheering for you.

Facebook is not only seen as a site for friends, it can also be used as a powerful business tool. It's a perfect venue to promote your books and connect with your readers. It's important to have a personal page and a fan page. Some authors only have a fan page while others only have a personal page. What works for you may not work for others and you are the best judge to see what works for you.

Facebook can be used to connect with other authors like you. There are various group pages you can participate in that make you feel you're a member of a community. What better way to discuss and share information in a group? You can build relationships and support one another. There are Facebook pages that allow authors to post their book daily for free. There are other pages that share books daily to their 100,000 followers. Even if you get 10% of followers, you've made quite an achievement.

Facebook is a visual site where people can post and share photos, links and information. What I like most about Facebook is the interaction I get from people. News spreads fast on Facebook, and this is a perfect place to announce your new book. Again, it's not about hard selling your book but using a creative way to promote your work.

From my experience, most of my readers and fans like to see a personal side of me. My achievements and announcements are always exciting news for them, but showing other personal matters add equal value. There was one time I sprained my ankle and posted a photo of my cast with a witty blurb saying no more dancing and high heels for me. I generated a lot of comments and people engaged in a conversation. Another time I posted a photo that I won two gift cards a Christmas party raffle and that also generated comments. What I'm trying to point out is that you can share ordinary situations. Authors are humans and the way for authors and readers to really connect is to show a personal side.

Since social media is about generosity, don't be stingy in liking and commenting on other people's photos and links. This is a perfect way to engage in a conversation and to generate new readers.

What I also like about Facebook is being able to help one another. My high school batch has their own group page where we can post photos, share the latest pictures and announcements and ask for information. The page is only for all our batchmates to see. Last year, one of our batchmates was in the hospital due to a kidney disease. She had two kidney transplants and was in her end stage. Her family was not only grieving but overwhelmed with hospital bills they had to shoulder. We pulled together and were able to raise enough money to pay for her hospital bills and even had extra. We would not have been able to do this if we were not a part of Facebook.

There was a massive typhoon that struck the Philippines. The support that was given has been phenomenal. People working together to send funds and relief goods proved that the spirit of humanity still exists. Facebook has such a huge platform, and connecting with people to support a good cause unites us.

Creating a banner for your Facebook cover page is a wonderful opportunity to display your work. Don't hold back in liking and commenting on other people's pictures and posts. People love to interact.

Twitter:

Twitter is another online social network that offers microblogging services. Since Twitter only allows 140 characters, you have to keep your posts short. Twitter works differently from Facebook but is a powerful tool for authors.

Twitter can make or break you. With 140 characters you need to ensure you have an attractive Bio. Use key words that allow people to find you. This is the Bio I put on Twitter. Best-selling, award-winning Romance and Women's fiction Author of *Love Letters*, *Chocolicious* and *The Assignment* which are being adapted into film. If you'll notice. I provide all the information about my books.

Twitter works to your advantage when you know how to leverage your tweets. Someone new to Twitter may get overwhelmed and not know what to do. I often hear people say, it's lonely here and what am I supposed to tweet about. Follow people that interest you and they are most likely to follow you back. Twitter works differently from Facebook, but you can connect with a lot of people in a different level.

Looking for content to share on Twitter shouldn't be difficult if you know where to find them. As an author, you ought to keep yourself informed with what's happening with the publishing industry. You can search for informative resources to find quality content. The New York Times and The Huffington Post offer a lot of valuable information.

Our parents taught us not to speak to strangers, but the virtual world works differently. We can turn strangers into fans and friends. There's no specific rule with Twitter, but my strategy is to follow everyone who follows me. In my early stages of Twitter, I only wanted to follow people I knew or those where I could get vital information. I have to admit I was shy to talk to strangers and didn't engage much in a conversation. You would want to follow authors and their followers, literary agents, publishers, publicists, editors, book reviewers, book lovers and everyone connected to writing, editing, publishing and promoting.

I read a lot of blogs about writing and I would always post links to these blogs. I know my followers pay attention to my posts because they are often retweeted and added to their favorite list of tweets. If you read an article you find interesting, definitely tweet about it. Create a banner and have a nice headshot photo. I have three novels so my Twitter banner displays my three books.

Hashtags and Why They're Important:

People new to Twitter often wonder what hashtags are. One of the popular hashtags in the writing industry is #amwriting. If you were to use that hashtag before the article you posted, people are most likely to find you when searching for that hashtag. Posting without using hashtags will limit you from finding followers.

Popular Hashtags:
#amwriting
#mywana
#writerwednesday
#writetip
#wordcount

#followfriday
#fridayreads
#writingprompts
#askagent
#bookgiveaways

Link Shortener is a Must:
Twitter only has 140 characters, and you often find that the website where you read that phenomenal article is too long. Don't lose heart, you can always use a link shortener like bit.ly to shrink the link The idea is to leave enough space so people can retweet (RT) your tweets.

Scheduling Tweets a Week in Advance:
I schedule my tweets a week in advance, and it's usually every Sunday. I go through all the articles I've read from the different blogs, newspapers, and magazines I've visited and add them to my whole week of tweets. There are programs that you can use to schedule your tweets. HootSuite or Tweetdeck. When I started promoting my book, I would use Twitter daily and would schedule my tweets every three hours a day. I did this straight for six months, and it proved to be effective.

80 Percent Content and 20 Percent Promotion:
My rule of thumb is to give more than what I can get. If you're offering people substantial information that will help them grow their career, then they will pay attention to you. They'll see your Bio and most likely buy your books. I promote my books 1-2 times a day, and the way I do it is by

including the reviews written by my readers. This provides an indirect approach of promoting your book. Another creative way to promote your work is to use themes from your book. For Love Letters a sample tweet would be, #amwriting #mywana A story about second chances. For Chocolicious, #amwriting #chocolate A story about love, loss and redemption. For The Assignment, my tweet was #romance #mystery A story about love, betrayal and forgiveness. Notice how the themes are mentioned. Readers can gain an insight with these terms.

Have you ever heard of a Tweet chat? It is a set of live tweets from different people who post about the same topic using a specific hashtag. If you're coordinating a book launch, you can ask your team or friends to tweet about your new release at a certain date and time. This creates an effective way for your followers to participate and engage themselves.

If you follow a lot of people on Twitter, keeping track of their tweets can be overwhelming. You still want to keep up to date with important information, and one way to do this is to do hashtag search. You can track a lot of topics from the popular hashtags. Another way to be on track with important tweets is to sign up for Paper.li. Paper.li is your own customized newspaper that extracts all the important Twitter feeds from those you follow and delivers it via email. You get to read the news at your own leisure time. Paper.li only delivers significant updates daily, cutting out the spam. This is a free service. Don't be stingy in retweeting and favoriting other people's posts. You can also join www.worldliterarycafe.com and be a part of their

Tweet Team.

GoodReads:
GoodReads is a growing social network for readers and authors. This is an online site where you can hear about the latest books and read reviews from readers. What a great opportunity to display your books. GoodReads creates lists like Best Romance book, Best lead character, Best Summer Read, etc, and this allows readers to nominate you and vote for your books.

The site also has online forums that you can be a part of. Online forums allow you to share information, discuss about the latest book you've read and also build relationships with readers and authors.

GoodReads provides a venue for authors to schedule book giveaways. When launching your book, you can schedule the dates when you plan your give-away and this will allow readers to sign up ahead of time. Readers who win will post an honest review of your book and this will spread the word to their followers.

GoodReads also offers quizzes, trivia and quotes. What I've found very effective is using quotes from my novels. I never knew about this perk that GoodReads offered until I saw my quotes listed there. My readers were the ones who actually posted the quotes. Ever since they did that, I've seen so many blogs use my quote. People have also posted these quotes on Twitter. The popular quotes they've used come from my novel, Chocolicious. One of them states, "May your life be filled, as mine has been, with love and laughter; and remember, when things are rough all you need is ... Chocolate." I also see Chocolate boutiques that use my quote and post it on their blogs or on Facebook.

GoodReads also allows authors to use ads to promote their books. I personally have not used their ads, so I can't comment if it's effective.

YouTube:

Although YouTube isn't considered a social media, I believe that the site provides equal exposure to authors. One advantage for YouTube is that it allows authors to post a book trailer of their book. Book trailers are similar to movie trailers that feature sneak previews of your story. A book trailer can be costly, but authors can do it themselves with the help of online websites like www.animoto.com. There are online sites that provide free stock photos and free royalty music. You can post your book trailers on your website.

Instagram:

I recently started using Instagram and getting familiar with how this site works. Instagram seems like Twitter but features photos and videos. Instagram is more visual but you can also use hashtags to promote your photos and connect with readers and fans.

Other social media sites include Google Plus, Pinterest, LinkedIn and others. I don't use these sites, but I know many authors who have been successful using them. The idea is to not get overwhelmed but to use these sites productively to build your platform and have fun doing it.

www.klout.com measures your online presence and how influential you are in social media. The higher your score, the greater your presence.

If you're still unfamiliar on how Social Media works, I would recommend the following books:

Social Media Just For Writers

Facebook for Dummies

Twitter for Dummies

You can also take up short courses about social media and building your platform on
http://www.fostering-success.com/author-courses

Chapter 14
The X Factor in eBook Pricing

I sell more eBooks than paperbacks and most of my marketing strategies have increased my eBook sales.

Consider this, you are a new author and nobody but your group of friends including your ninth grade English teacher knows that you wrote a book. What will entice a reader to buy your eBook? Sure, you have an attractive cover and exciting summary but the price is $4.99. Next please! But with the $0.99 price point, you're surely capable of winning a few readers. That's even less than a cup of coffee. And if they like your book, you can guarantee they will talk about it.

Most of the Indie best-sellers have priced their eBooks to $0.99. You won't make much in royalties, but you'll gain lots of exposure. You can raise the price back to your original price after your promotions have been completed. This strategy helps market your other books wherein one book can be priced $.99 and the rest is $2.99

For traditionally published authors, you can work with your publisher and ask them if they can do a campaign for a few days or weeks with this price point. Readers are always looking for a bargain and a $0.99 price point can be very attractive. You might think that a low price devalues your work but bear in mind that a promo shouldn't last long.

When I did my campaign for *Love Letters* and *Chocolicious*, I was hesitant to lower my price to $0.99 but soon I noticed how effective this price point was for other authors. The minute I changed my price to $0.99 and did a full promotion, that's when both my books made it to the overall top 100 eBook bestseller list on Amazon. I knew then that pricing really matters and although I didn't make much in royalties, my goal was exposure and reaching more readers and fans.

Chapter 15
Why Advertisements Matter

James Patterson, the highest earning author, paid $6M in ads. Yes, that's right, $6M. I wish I had one tenth of his advertising budget so I can pay for ads. Ask yourself why Coca Cola, McDonalds, and Nike earn so much in revenue. They credit their exposure to ads. I'm sure a majority of you are saying, but I'm just a starving writer and don't have the funds to pay for ads. I understand your situation and not everybody has the budget to pay for ads, but I won't be a hypocrite and say that ads don't help you sell. Ads are investments you make as an author. You may not acquire back the investment, but you can guarantee you'll get exposure. If possible, set a budget and invest in ads every three months.

As authors, we can't do everything ourselves and most of these advertising companies have a wider platform and network then we do. If we tap into their network, we can reach more people and gain exposure.

Ads:
http://www.authorbuzz.com/
http://kindlenationdaily.com/
www.bookbub.com/
http://ereadernewstoday.com/
http://www.pixelofink.com/
www.GoodReads.com
http://www.manicreaders.com/
http://www.authorisland.com/

Chapter 16
A Newsletter is Your Highlight for the Month

As your career grows, you learn to start building your database of readers, and one way of updating them with your developments is through a newsletter. Consider emailing a newsletter every month that highlights the latest news in your career. You can advise your loyal fans about your next book.

Newsletters are more professional then just emailing everyone that you have a book coming out. Most authors send out a monthly newsletter pointing out the highlights of their work. It is especially useful if they are coming out with a new book or have an event they wish to share. Newsletters should not only be sent to your friends and family but to the readers who have also emailed you about your work.

There are free companies that offer these services. You can use their templates to customize your work.

Always add your email signature when you send out emails which include your website, Facebook, Twitter and other social media pages where people can find you. Even if you send emails to other people who aren't related to writing, they will most likely know someone who will be interested in your work.

Resources:
Mailchimp
Constant Contact

Chapter 17
Who Doesn't Love Freebies

A lot of famous authors are offering free eBooks on Amazon and other venues. Now tell me, who doesn't want a free book? I'm sure we all get excited when we see a great bargain, but free offers a better deal. A month ago, best-selling author Barbara Freethy offered her book for free on Amazon. I immediately downloaded a copy on my Kindle and read the book in two days. Not only did I fall in love with her book, but I also purchased her other novels.

I decided to try this free promo with *Love Letters*. I kept the free promos for two days and I gained over 25,000 downloads. That's 25,000 new readers who have heard about me. This tactic compliments you even more if you have other books. I received a ton of fan mail in two days from my readers, and this helped build my author's platform. When I reverted back to the original price, the sales soared. Since this strategy has worked for me, I have committed myself to doing this every three months. This has proven to be effective especially since your book appears in the free category best-seller list on Amazon.

Amazon's algorithms kick in and your book becomes more visible. Amazon recommends your books to their readers based on the books they've purchased. You will see the term, "Customers who bought this item also bought…" You'll notice the ripple effect in a few days when you've changed back to the original price, and your readers will also start purchasing your other books.

There are various sites that will feature your free promo by posting on their blog, Facebook and Twitter.

Sites to promote your free book:
www.bookbub.com/
http://ereadernewstoday.com/
http://www.pixelofink.com/
http://ebookdealofday.com/
http://ebookshabit.com/
http://freekindleebooks.com/
http://www.addictedtoebooks.com/node?page=1019
http://bargainebookhunter.com/
http://digitalbooktoday.com/
http://freebooksy.com/

Chapter 18
The Power of Amazon

Amazon is changing the way readers read and connect and the way books get published. Thanks to Amazon, authors can instantly publish their work. Authors should take advantage of the opportunities Amazon has to offer. Amazon allows you to classify your books in genres and sub-genres. One useful tip is to use sub-genres that are not common.

My third novel, The Assignment, is set internationally in the Philippines. The book's genre is a cross-over between a historical romance with a touch of mystery and drama. If I were to classify *The Assignment* as a historical novel, then my novel would get lost in the crowd of books. Instead I chose to define the genre as specific as possible—Literature & Fiction > Drama & Plays > Asian.

In light of this strategy, I am able to gain more exposure, and this has allowed my novel to be a best-seller in this category. Authors need to choose a specific genre and sub-genre to be able to appear in Amazon's list.

Every author should have an Amazon Central page that features a professional headshot photo and an attractive Bio. Most readers who come across your books want to know the author behind the book. The summary of your book should also be captivating enough for readers to want to read more.

Amazon allows readers to post reviews which helps boost sales. New authors are hungry to gain reviews for their books. One effective way to do this is when you schedule your virtual blog tour. The blog hosts who read your books and post reviews on their site are also kind enough to post their reviews on Amazon. If you've also done giveaways, you can request the winners to post an honest review.

Chapter 19
Don't Be Intimidated by Online Writing Communities and Forums

An online forum is where people can post a discussion in the form of messages. Anybody can participate in an online forum and this way of communication has proven to be effective. An author should consider being a part of an online writing community. Online forums only prove that you're not alone. Online forums can assist new authors gain first-hand information about certain topics. You may be looking for a graphic artist to do your book cover and what better way then to ask for referrals? You may need advice for an idea about the plot of your book or need the support of other authors.

We've all heard of successful stories of authors connecting with readers and writers on the Kindleboards. If you have time and enjoy talking to other people, this can be very effective. Forums are not a place to push and promote your book. Forums are meant for authors and aspiring authors to discuss, share some tips, chat about the latest trends or simply make friends. This is how you build relationships with other authors and readers.

Each and every one of us has information to share or is an expert in our field. Forums are all about give and take. Sharing tips and information is one way for people to get to know you. If you help others, they will want to support you and one way to do that is by buying your book.

Online forum sites:
www.GoodReads.com
www.kindleboards.com
www.worldliterarycafe.com

Chapter 20
Cross-Promotions with Other Authors Build Synergy

I'm sure you're familiar with the saying that two heads are better than one, and this also applies to promoting your book. Writing can be a solitary experience as we spend days toiling away on our computer. Thanks to the internet and social media, I've met a whole bunch of versatile authors. Two years ago, a group of us banded together to support an author with her book launch. All of us offered a special promo of selling our books for $0.99 only—thirty six books for $0.99. Great deal, right? Definitely not one you'd find everyday.

Despite living in different parts of the world, we managed to communicate daily, sharing one goal—to help one another succeed. We all worked hard to promote one another on Facebook, Twitter and other social media networks. We conducted author interviews, guest blogs and shared book reviews, all in the hope to create buzz for the book launch and to let the people know who we are. But that wasn't all . . . As the days began to unfold, a strong bond developed between us, and we didn't only see ourselves as authors who wrote and promoted books, but as humans who savored friendship. The relationship we have has allowed us to share our days of triumphs and voice out our frustrations.

A listening ear, a praise, and a kind word reassured us that we would always be there for each other through thick and thin. It was one for all, and all for one—a commitment we all made and kept. We worked hard to create buzz, and on the day itself, everybody sold more books than they sold in a month and benefited from the event. That event revealed the power of synergy and working together as a team. You can find authors like you through social media, blogs, forums, online writer's communities. We all need one another and should never be alone.

One way to do this is to use Twitter, Facebook, online writing communities or other group pages you are a part of to find authors who you can partner with. Many new authors are searching for authors like you to be a bigger part of a community. Another advantage is if you can request authors to write a blurb and review of your book. You can post the blurbs on Amazon, your book cover and your website.

Chapter 21
Joining Contests Provide Exposure

There are so many online contests that authors can participate in. You have to make sure you do your due diligence when searching for a legitimate contest. Some contests require a fee while others don't. The prices they offer may not be worth much but you're after the exposure. When I released my debut novel, *Love Letters* I joined two contests and I won the Beach Book Festival and flew to New York to receive my certificate. *Love Letters* also made it to Finalist for the Global eBook Awards. I recently won the Agent's Pick for IPR License and got a fine critique by a UK literary agent.

Winning an award is a magical experience and winning one allows you to add to your Bio that you are an award-winning author. The more awards you win, the better for your Bio and leverage.

Contests:
http://www.writersdigest.com/competitions/writing-competitions
http://globalebookawards.com/
http://beachbookfestival.com/
http://www.bulwer-lytton.com/
http://www.beforecolumbusfoundation.com/
http://www.glimmertrain.com/
http://www.penusa.org/awards
http://www.pen-ne.org/
http://indieexcellence.com/
http://www.hofferaward.com/
http://www.independentpublisher.com/ipland/IPAwards.php

Chapter 22
Build a Following

What butter is to bread, are what readers are to books. They are the blood passing through your veins, and without them, where will you be? You can't only rely on your friends and family. You need a lot more readers. You want them to carry a piece of you with them. Do you realize that every reader who reads your book means you have made an impact on them? They took the time to purchase the book, read it, and built an impression. Whether they loved your work or hated your story, you still allowed them to feel something about your book. I believe that's the most magical thing for an author. You may not know that reader, and the reader may live miles away from you, but at some point in time, you had connected with your readers through your story.

How do you connect with your readers? Write more books. Writers enjoy writing, and for me it's still the best job in the world. Writing comes naturally to me, while marketing, on the other hand, involves a different ball game, which not only takes skill, talent and creativity, but guts and determination.

Chapter 23
Time Management is Significant

We live in a highly fast-paced world where people demand everything with a push of a button, where we are over-scheduled and sleep deprived. I for one hate schedules because deadlines can ruin my creativity. However, I need to set time during the day to write and promote my books. I have a full-time job, family and activities, and balancing writing and promoting in between can feel like working a second job. People often ask me how I juggle everything, and my answer is, I just do it. People who know me well enough will agree that I am always on the go and my determination to succeed is what keeps me moving forward.

Now that you've learned all the strategies I've used, you can mark your planner and set a to-do list. List down your short-term and long-term goals. Ask yourself in terms of platform, what you want to achieve in the next six months or so. You know yourself and you know what will work best for you, so stick to your goal.

Chapter 24
Be Consistent and Write More Books

You've done your homework, and you've been receiving a lot of fan emails, you've sold some books, and most importantly, you've already built your platform, so what's next? You're in the middle of writing another book, but want to keep the momentum, right? The key is to be consistent. The reason why Nicholas Sparks, James Patterson, and Danielle Steel continue to have loyal fans following them, is because readers know what to expect. Can you imagine if Stephen King writes a romance novel and stopped living up to his image? What a great loss that would be.

Unless you wrote *Gone with the Wind* and had a lifetime achievement, not many readers will hear about you. If readers are hungry for your first book, they'll most likely want to grab a copy of your second, your third, and so forth. Some authors prefer to write a series and this strategy has proven to be successful like *Harry Potter*, *Twilight* and *Fifty Shades of Grey*. Now that you have people who have heard about you, read your books, and are craving to read more, you need to let them develop their trust in you. Give them the confidence that you will deliver, that you will write another breakout novel, that you will teach something and that you will always leave them hungry for more.

Yet how do you balance writing, promoting and still have a life? The author's life never stops. You are constantly managing writing, publishing and promoting. Now that you've worked hard to build your author's platform, you will notice a ripple effect. This doesn't usually happen right away. This may take months or even a year or so to witness the results, but you'll be amazed that all your hard work has paid off. I intensely promoted my books for three consecutive months then continued the momentum for a whole year. I scheduled a break when I began writing my third book. I have to be honest that I felt overwhelmed trying to juggle both. I needed to focus and nurture my creative side.

What surprised me most, was that despite taking a break, my platform didn't dwindle. I thought readers and fans had forgotten about me, but I was mistaken. This was the most exciting time of my career where now other people were the ones talking about me and my books. How did I learn about this? One tool was to sign up for Google Alerts where you can manage if people are talking about you and your books. Google will keep track and email you notifications when there is news about you.

Through Google alerts I was notified that

people were talking about my books they read on online forums. I also discovered people using quotes of my books on their blogs, with my name of course. A lady posted a picture of a paperback copy of my novel, *Chocolicious* on Twitter and said that she had just completed reading my book. I thanked her and asked her how she heard about my book. She informed me that she came across *Chocolicious* at a Singapore library. I was surprised to find out that my novel was available in Singapore when I never donated a copy to the Singapore library. I was so delighted that I asked if she can write me an honest review on Amazon. She did and after reading *Chocolicious*, she bought my two other books.

On Facebook, I found many people posting photos of my books and telling their friends about me. I also started receiving emails almost daily from fans who have read my books. This brought a smile to my face and only reminded me that all my efforts were not wasted. When this happens always thank your readers and fans for supporting you. Their loyalty goes a long way and they are always honored when you appreciate them.

Chapter 25
Celebrate Your Milestones

You've worked hard to build your platform in your pajamas and have reached a wide audience for your book. Now comes the time to celebrate your milestones. Don't be shy to share this with your virtual followers and friends. You've earned your status and you deserve the best. Open a bottle of champagne and make a toast to your hard work. Keep a log of all your achievements and awards and take every photo to cherish the memories. Even the smallest of your milestones should be celebrated.

I only sold five books in the first month, but I told myself that this was only the beginning of my journey. I knew I was in this ride for the long haul and was ready and committed to do everything it takes to build my author's platform. I've come a long way from where I've started, but I will always remember my humble beginnings. There is no ending to an author's journey. My goal is to inspire, educate, entertain and touch many readers in one lifetime. Every moment counts and I want to provide a legacy for generations to come.

Celebrate your milestones and reward yourself for all the hard work and determination. I'm a firm believer in the three P's which are Passion, Perseverance and Prayer. This mantra keeps me going. Writing this book is my way of giving back and encouraging authors that they can build their platform.

Disclosure

All the 25 chapters I wrote were steps that helped me build my author's platform. What worked for me may not necessarily work for you which is why I always advice new authors to conduct their research and due diligence. When you read this book, please note that some links may not be active since websites could change from time to time.

In this regard, I hope you've found this book to be helpful and beneficial to your writing career.

Acknowledgements

First and foremost, I would like to thank all the readers and fans that have supported me throughout my career. Without you guys, there will be no authors like me. You have continued to motivate me to write powerful stories that can inspire, educate and entertain many readers like you.

A heartfelt thanks to my editor and book formatter, Rachelle Ayala who has intricately brought my book within publishing standards. You are so flexible to work with and have a smile that could light up any room.

Thank you to my cover artist, Anna Price who not only created a stellar cover but worked to my specifications. You are so talented and deserve to be recognized.

To Dawn Armstrong, Beth Barany, and Linda Lysakowski for providing insights and ideas for this book.

A million thanks to my publicist, Danny Deraney of Deraney Publications who has helped me reach a broader audience and opened more doors for me. You totally rock!

To my darling husband, Arnel Solon, and sweet son, Stefan Solon, for always understanding the solitude I needed to complete this book and for always supporting me with my work.

Last and not least, to God Almighty for all the abundant blessings.

About the Author

Geraldine Solon is the award-winning, best-selling author of three novels—*Love Letters, Chocolicious and The Assignment.* Two of her books have been adapted into film. Geraldine is the Managing Editor of food/fashion/lifestyle magazine, Gastronomique en Vogue She is also the Vice President of the Fremont Area Writers club and the Screenwriter/Executive producer of her upcoming movie, Love Letters. Geraldine has studied creative writing and screenwriting courses at Stanford University. She is currently working on a screenplay.

www.ingramcontent.com/pod-product-compliance
Lightning Source LLC
Chambersburg PA
CBHW051815170526
45167CB00005B/2027